MY
Hospital
Story

Nell Choi

BALBOA.PRESS

A DIVISION OF HAY HOUSE

Balboa Press books may be ordered through booksellers or by contacting:

Balboa Press
A Division of Hay House
1663 Liberty Drive
Bloomington, IN 47403
www.balboapress.com
844-682-1282

Cover Design by Nerissa Baroni

Print information available on the last page.

ISBN: 978-1-9822-6284-6 (sc)
ISBN: 978-1-9822-6285-3 (e)

Balboa Press rev. date: 01/29/2021

I am donating 100% of the proceeds from the sales of this book to the Neurohospitalist Reasearch Fund SPF 44526 at Children's National Hospital. This fund will advance research and care for patients with neuroinflammatory/ neuroimmune conditions, including NMOSD (neuromyelitis optica spectrum disease).

I dedicate this book to Ms. Helen Poon, for her amazing courage and making everything fun.

When you come out of the storm, you won't be the same person that walked in.

That's what the storm is all about.

—Haruki Murakami

This is a note written to me by my older brother, Jake, when he was thirteen years old:

Dear Nell,

Today is your infusion. Everyone is going to say the same thing to you; be brave ; be strong. However, I am going to say something different to you; be yourself. You do not need to change anything to become brave ; you already are. Your cheerful personality will always allow you to combat fear. You must accept who you are. You are Ms Nello Choi, and nothing, I repeat nothing can stop your drive and brightness.

Good Luck Today,

Jake Choi

CONTENTS

Introduction

Have you ever felt like your life was suddenly taken away from you, and you were banished and trapped in another world? Well, I have. My name is Nell, and I'm twelve years old. A few years ago in February 2018, I was in the hospital for nearly a month. I was nine then. It all happened very suddenly—the sickness, I mean. In early January, I was loving life: skiing in Steamboat, Colorado, with my family; gliding down fluffy white snow mountains with my big brother Jake; and then sipping hot chocolate on a big soft couch in front of a warm, crackling fireplace in the lodge.

Then *bam!* When I got back home, I developed a mysterious sickness with belly pain and nausea, which we all thought was the flu—until we knew it wasn't.

My symptoms weren't getting better, and I even started to develop weirder symptoms, like dizziness and extreme fatigue. I seriously wanted to sleep all the time. I finally went to the emergency room, where doctors discovered through an MRI inflammation in my brain, and quite a lot of it, which they diagnosed as a rare autoimmune disease. That discovery was the start of my long hospital experience. Who would have known that fateful day that I entered the emergency room would lead to nearly an entire month of my life spent in a hospital bed and then another year fighting to get my old life back?

To make a long story short, I never really got my old life back. I mean, I did *eventually* get better— that's how I'm writing this book—but I have a new life now. In some ways it's better. Let me explain.

Don't get me wrong: being in the hospital, away from my friends, with all sorts of needles in my arm and tubes up my nose and suffering through endless respiratory treatments was just plain *awful*. Even after fighting those battles, I had to relearn how to walk, write, and pick up my lacrosse stick.

It was a fight mentally and physically, but the mental obstacles were the toughest to overcome. I wondered if I was ever going to play lacrosse or return to school and be a normal student again.

It was especially hard because I knew nobody could really understand what I was feeling, not even my amazing friends or my loving family. When talking to my family about some of my sad and angry feelings didn't help, I expressed them through writing. My journaling became a sort of secret weapon for me to combat all of the frustration I was feeling. When I wrote, the pencil moved and my thoughts flowed onto the paper, transforming my negative thoughts into positive ones. I felt a little better each time I wrote, and eventually, I started to understand how much I gained from this challenging experience.

In addition to how I helped myself, I received help from those surrounding me. They were the people who went a little or a lot out of their way to help me, pray for me, or just think about me. They were family, friends, teachers, coaches, nurses, doctors, physical and occupational therapists, and so many more, including people who didn't even know me but heard about my situation. These people were my angels—not the kind with halos above their heads and wings, but actual people.

I discovered so many angels through this whole experience. I'd like to be an angel to you, just as others were to me. I hope that the story of my battle will inspire you to keep fighting and that my triumphs will give you the strength you need to succeed. Thank you for reading my book.

Day 1: **I Enter the Storm**

Happiness can be found in the
darkest of times, if one only
remembers to turn on the light.

—Dumbledore

When I arrive at the emergency room on a cold evening in January, my doctors order an MRI test. My tired body is pushed into a dark, narrow tunnel where I hear pounding and knocking sounds. The loud noises penetrate my earplugs even though my head is squished between cushion holders. My hands are cold and sweaty. I want to scream, but I don't. An unfamiliar voice tells me to lie very still. He's the MRI technologist, and he needs to get good pictures of my brain. An MRI (magnetic resonance imaging) machine is a big machine that uses magnets and a computer to take images of the inside of your body.

1

So I hold still in this loud, dark tunnel. I am confused and exhausted. My eyelids grow heavy, feeling like huge sacks. Memories flash through my mind: the emergency room, doctors hovering over me, nurses connecting wires and tubes all over my body, lots of beeping sounds, a million questions, and chaos.

When I wake up, I don't hear the loud noises anymore. I am on a moving bed, being wheeled through endless hallways by strangers. My eyes dart back and forth to make sense of my surroundings. My heart starts to pound. My mind races with questions: *Where am I? Where is my mom? Where are they taking me?*

When my eyes finally meet my mom's, I'm so relieved. I ask, "Where are we now?"

My mom looks at me sympathetically and says, "Nell, you are being admitted to the hospital." A wave of fear washes over me. Looking at my finger that is taped up to a wire that checks my pulse, I know this is true. Then, another wave of emotion washes over me: sadness. As that wave crashes down upon me, tears like big raindrops well up in my eyes and roll down my cheeks. Everything is blurry.

I wonder how long I will be here. Why do I need to be here? What is Jake, my brother, doing at home? Is he cuddling with Bunnis, our sweet bunny? I want to be there with them. What are my friends doing at school? Are they running around on the playground, having fun without me? I want to be there, too. As these thoughts race through my mind, I feel the warmth of Mom's body as she wraps her arms around me. "Mom, do I have to stay in the hospital because of something bad they found on my MRI scans?" I ask anxiously. She sits down on the bed and draws in a deep breath.

"Yes, Nell, but the doctors aren't sure what it all means yet. That's why we're going to stay in the hospital for a little while—to sort it out." I still have questions, but I can tell my mom doesn't want to talk about it. So I nod and stare up at the ceiling from my stretcher, wishing this could all be a bad dream. My body aches with exhaustion, so I close my eyes and fall asleep.

Reflection

I was really scared that day. Nobody knew what was going on. There was so much confusion. We finally got answers after my mom's doctor friend in radiology fit me into the packed MRI schedule. He stayed at the hospital late that night to review my MRI scan carefully. I didn't realize it then, but without him, our confusion would have been even more intense. He was one of my first angels. Before that day, I was a super healthy kid, an ambitious student, and a travel lacrosse player. Going to the hospital and getting that MRI completely changed my life. But it was only the start of my long journey.

Week 1: **The Whiteboard**

The more you are in a state of
gratitude, the more you will
attract things to be grateful for.

—Walt Disney

I spend most of my time in the hospital sleeping. Days pass, and I don't even notice. My mom, dad, and older brother, Jake, come to visit me regularly. They look tired and worried but try to hide it. Jake is two years older than me, so he's eleven. He holds my hand and tells me funny stories about Bunnis, our sweet chubby bunny. He reminds me of the time we fed her cherries, and they turned her whole mouth bright red, making her look like she was wearing lipstick. I laugh. I'm glad Jake is here. I wish I could hold Bunnis now.

My most frequent visitors are doctors, who ask me many of the same questions and listen to my heart and lungs and poke around my body. I wonder why they can't all come at once so they don't keep waking me up and wasting time repeating themselves. They all look worried but don't say much. I'm still so tired that I drift into sleep midconversation. The difference between day and night becomes less clear. Each time I wake up, I don't know what time of day it is.

At first, I don't even care about the doctors visiting, but after they all start waking me up and groping and poking my body, it becomes too much. First it's the nurse, then the head neurologist wakes me up midsleep, then the nurse again, then the neurologist in training (they call him the resident), and then the pulmonologist startles me when he puts a cold, round stethoscope on my chest to listen to me breathe, and finally the ophthalmologist enters to examine my eyes. By now, I am waiting for the lady with the alligator purse! This became a daily routine for me.

Because I start to feel overwhelmed by the unpredictable flow of people coming in and out of my room, Mom suggests creating a schedule for each day on a whiteboard hanging on the wall that faces my bed. It lets me know when doctors or visitors will be seeing me and when I can rest. Only family is allowed to visit for now. I like this whiteboard idea because knowing what to expect in my day makes me feel less anxious. Just because I'm not at school doesn't mean I don't have the right to know my daily schedule!

One day, I wake up to see my mom writing on the whiteboard. I ask her, "Mom, which doctor will be seeing me today?"

5

"Today you will be seeing the pulmonologist and the neurologist," she replies softly. I nod my head and wonder what is going on at school. I wish I could be with my friends, go to my classes, and learn new things. I wonder what is going on in my homeroom. Maybe they are doing more work on global education, playing a new math game, or dancing to "Funky Town" when they have to clean up. Whenever I hear that song and that funky beat, I start dancing. I just can't help it. I wonder if my friends miss me. I definitely miss them.

Reflection

I'm grateful to my family for being with me during this time and to my mom for knowing that the whiteboard would help structure my day a little more. Knowing what would happen next was important to me so I could mentally prepare. The schedule helped me feel calmer amid the chaos of the hospital.

Week 2: **Torture Devices**

> The mind is everything. What
> you think, you become.
>
> —Buddha

Over the course of the second week, there are several troubling developments. First, breathing became very difficult. I remember my dad's worried face (picture your dad's expression as he sucks on a Warhead sour candy). I gasp for air because the saliva clogs up my throat; it feels like I'm drowning. Because of my weakened breathing, I have a tube called a nasal cannula that blows more oxygen placed in my nose. I am weaker, so my doctors order respiratory treatments to help me with my breathing. I absolutely despise these treatments. They are really torture devices that are dubbed treatments. One of my torture devices is a vibrating vest the nurse puts on my chest. It's supposed to help move the mucus out of my lungs. Every few hours, I have to suffer ten minutes of pure misery, shaking and coughing uncontrollably.

I also have trouble eating, so they put a feeding tube up my nose and down into my stomach. I won't state the obvious and tell you that this is very uncomfortable and I hate it, but I guess I just did. Let's leave it at that.

Because my tongue is weak, I also have trouble talking. I become frustrated because nobody can understand me, and I have to repeat myself over and over. I am so tired of this. Seeing my frustration with verbal communication, my mom hands me a whiteboard, but I realize my right arm has also become weak. I can barely hold a marker in my hand, let alone write.

Now I have to use the bathroom, but I can't tell anyone. I look at my mom, and she understands. She calls for the nurse to help disconnect my wires from the pulse and oxygen monitors that hold me prisoner in my bed. Mom and the nurse lift me up out of bed and help walk me to the bathroom. Because it becomes so hard to get me to the bathroom, they suggest using a bedpan, which I flatly refused. That's a plastic bowl they put in your bed for you to pee into. They get me a bedside mini toilet called a commode instead. I'll spare you the details, which thankfully, I barely recall.

I can't believe I can't even go to the bathroom by myself. "What is happening to me?" I want to scream at the top of my lungs, but I am too weak. Tears stream down my face, but I can't wipe them off. Everything is blurry, and I'm exhausted. I fade into a deep sleep.

Reflection

I don't remember that time in the hospital very well, which is probably a good thing. I remember feeling tired and scared, really scared. I didn't know it then, but it was the lowest point in my hospital journey. Maybe you have to hit rock bottom before you can pull yourself back up again, but you have to believe you can. I leaned on my mom and all of my caregivers and tried my best to believe that things would be okay.

Week 3, Day 1: **Distinguished Honor Roll**

> If you light a lamp for someone else,
> it will also brighten your path.

> —Buddha

Because I'm in the hospital all this time, people start to worry. Since they can't visit me yet, my friends drop off cards bursting with kind words of hope, love, and support. I read comments like, "Get well, Nell! We miss your smile and laugh. You got this!" that fill my heart with so much joy. I miss my friends, my teachers, and my lacrosse teammates and coaches so much. I hate being stuck in this room, in this horrible place! Though these notes give me a lift, I still feel a deep hole in my heart. I want to have my old life back.

I feel alone. It's quiet in my room, and I'm sitting in my recliner with an IV in my arm and the IV bag hanging beside me. It starts to beep, but nobody comes in to fix it. I don't care. I feel so tired and let my eyes close.

When I wake up, I hear the sound of two different voices, one of which is my mom's. When I look up, I see my aunt Mel! I haven't seen her in a very long time, since I was a toddler. I barely remember her.

"Hey, Nell, how ya doing?" she asks me. I look at her for a second, trying to remember her.

"Okay," I answer hesitantly and groggily, still trying to recall the last time I saw her. She nods and pulls out some food from her bag, which she hands to my mom. I bet my mom told her that I can't swallow very well because she doesn't offer me any. As they eat, I lean back in the recliner and watch commercials playing on the TV. Just as I am about to relax, a person wearing gray hospital scrubs enters. *Oh no*, I think. It's the respiratory torturer, yet again.

"Time for your next breathing treatment," she announces softly but firmly.

"Which one?" I grumble. She pulls out a mask and holds it up for me to see. I hate doing all of these breathing treatments so much that I shouldn't even care which one it is. They are all equally awful. But still, I know I have trouble breathing, so I try to cooperate and hope it helps. The nurse places a mask over my mouth that pushes air down my throat for ten seconds, making me cough up mucus. Imagine being suffocated for ten seconds: it feels like a lifetime. She repeats this a few times—a few lifetimes.

Aunt Mel knows I hate these treatments, so she turns on the Food Network, my favorite channel. Cooking and baking are two of my favorite activities, so this distraction makes me slightly less miserable. I smile when I realize the Kids Baking Championship is showing, and they are baking macarons, my favorite! One of the kids makes a macaron with Earl Gray tea—I wonder how they come up with these ideas. I look at Aunt Mel and smile "thank you." She understands, smiles back, and gives me a thumbs-up. That makes me feel warm and cozy inside. I realize how much I have missed her and how happy I am that she is back in my life.

After the treatments, we keep an eye on my oxygen saturation reading on the monitor. Ideally, it should be as close to 100 percent as possible, but mine is dipping down into the upper 80s. So Aunt Mel tells me to take a deep breath and cheers when my oxygen saturation reads 91 percent. She tells me I am on the honor roll and encourages me to take more deep breaths. When I reach 97 percent, she announces that I qualify for the distinguished honor roll. I can't stop myself from smiling and giving her a thumbs-up. She's so funny.

Reflection

Hard times can bring friends and family closer. It seemed like when Aunt Mel was helping me, she was also happier. That was really special.

Week 3, Day 2: **Learning to Brush Again**

A single sunbeam is enough to
drive away many shadows.

—St. Francis of Assisi

It is February now. My walls are covered with cards written by my family and friends, teachers, and lacrosse teammates and coaches. I see stuffed animals, balloons, and books lining the windowsill and sitting on the table beside my bed. My friend Kayla sewed me a Chewbacca doll, which makes me smile because we have a secret joke about Chewbacca. It seems like so long ago.

Families take turns dropping off meals at my house for my brother and my parents because they are so busy visiting me at the hospital. Some of the meals are actually homemade and really delicious, as I hear from Jake. My friend Molly and her mom bake a chicken pot pie, and my friend Madison drops off beef-and-bean chili. Alana drops off brownies. I know they are all so worried about me, and I am sad that I am causing them all so much stress.

Today, I wake up to a knock on my door. I'm praying it's not the respiratory torturer because I just can't take another treatment right now. I hold my breath as the door slowly opens. Then I breathe a huge sigh of relief when I see Coach Kat standing in the doorway. I gasp with surprise and excitement as Kat's smile and energy fill my room with sunshine—and let me tell you, I'm talking about huge rays of sunshine. She gives me the biggest bear hug and says, "Hey, kid, what's up? How ya doing?" Kat is my lacrosse coach, and she is probably the most enthusiastic, energetic, and positive person I know.

"I'm okay. How's the team doing?" I ask her, but it sounds more like a gurgle because I can't swallow my saliva and my tongue muscles are weak. Despite that, Kat seems to understand me just fine and doesn't make me feel weird about my speech.

"They're doin' great! But everyone wishes they had their awesome defender there," she replies with a huge grin on her face. "Well, I brought some fun stuff for you, girl!" she announces as she pulls out a few things from her bag. My eyes grow wide with excitement as she pulls out fun coloring books, nail polish, a unicorn rug latch kit, and a giant rainbow unicorn Beanie Boo stuffed animal! Obviously, Kat loves unicorns.

As she places the unicorn in my arms, my mind flashes back to memories of Kat coaching me in lacrosse, encouraging me to be strong, and strengthening my resolve when I wanted to give up from frustration or fatigue. Here she is again, supporting me when I am at my lowest.

I don't know how she always knows when to show up in my life. She was by my side long before I was hospitalized. During a practice in early January, Kat noticed I was starting to feel weak and sick, and then she noticed I missed the next few practices. So she surprised me by showing up at my house with a box of personalized get-well cookies. I cried tears of joy when I saw her at my front door. I kept my special cookies in a container on my desk so I could look at them every day. They were the most beautifully decorated cookies I had ever seen, with smile emojis and "get well soon" written on them in red frosting. I had to admire them for a while before I ate them. I let Jake eat one right away, though, because I could tell he really wanted one.

Kat says she has something else for me, and she reaches into her bag and pulls out a toothbrush and toothpaste. "Even though you're here, you still need to take care of yourself," she advises. So for the next twenty minutes, Kat teaches me how to brush my teeth again. It is a little tricky since my right arm is especially weak, and I can barely even hold the toothbrush, let alone clean my teeth with it. I can't believe I have to relearn a skill that I could do without thinking as a toddler. That feels weird and scary, but Kat acts like it's no big deal. With her help, I do it. When I finally finish, it feels like a huge accomplishment.

I want Kat to stay longer, but I know I'm getting tired. I thank her for all of her gifts but know that her best gifts are the intangible ones: making me laugh, making me feel normal even when I have trouble brushing my teeth, and most of all, reminding me of my strength, both inside and out. When she is around me, I believe I will be strong and healthy again. Kat shares a secret: she is actually very afraid of hospitals and needles. Despite this, she visits me often.

After she gives me another huge bear hug, she tells me she will be back soon. She packs up her things and quietly closes the door behind her. As I close my eyes, I feel a new sense of hope that readies me for whatever lies ahead.

Reflection

I think Kat is definitely an angel. That she shows up in my life when I really need her makes me think so. Honestly, she's kind of magical. Helping me up when I'm down and being there to always cheer me on is something that makes her special. Not only that, but Kat pushes me to face my fears and gives me the courage to do so. She is my hero. To this day, I am grateful for her help and love.

Week 3, Day 3: **Costume Party?**

Good friends are like stars. You
don't always see them, but you
know they're always there.

—Unknown

I wake up to another knocking noise at my door. My eyes dart over to the clock and notice that it is 4:30 p.m. *Hmm, too early for the dinner tray.* I wonder who is supposed to come. When my mom opens the door, bright joyful voices instantly fill my room. They are the voices of two of my buddies from school, Rachel and Amelia. They're wearing their uniforms, so I know they came straight from school. But on top of their uniforms, they're wearing thin yellow gowns. In fact, everybody in the room, including my mom, Amelia's mom, and Rachel's au pair, Alissandra, are wearing yellow gowns.

I am drowsy and confused. "Uh, why is everyone wearing the yellow poncho-like outfits?" I ask my mom.

I'm hoping it's a costume party and they're all dressed up as the sun or something fun like that. Ha. Maybe I'm dreaming. I *would* rub my eyes, but that's right, I can't. I have a pulse monitor clipped to my finger and an IV sticking in my arm, and I'm still so weak. I won't bother. Anyway, nope, no such luck. My mom explains that I have a virus that might be contagious, so all of my visitors have to wear gowns to prevent them from catching or spreading this virus. I don't really understand that fully, but I am too distracted by the excitement of seeing my friends that I don't waste any more time discussing it.

My eyes instead fall onto the huge, colorful bags my friends are carrying.

"We brought you fun gifts," Amelia says, beaming.

"Yeah, and a good amount of them too!" Rachel cheers. They each reach into the bags and pull out something: a big, fluffy hamburger pillow and a cupcake squishy. I'm so happy. I feel like I've been transported back to a place that's full of fun, free from IV lines and wires tethering me to a hospital bed. I'm with my friends swimming and splashing around in a pool on a hot summer day. The water feels refreshingly cool on our skin as we float on our backs and feel the warm August sun on our faces.

I'm startled back to reality when Amelia's mom says, "Okay, Nell, when you're mad, throw that cupcake squishy across the room." I think, *Yes, I'll definitely have to do that.*

"And when you're *really* mad, throw that huge hamburger pillow," Rachel adds with a giggle. I smile and then burst into laughter with my friends.

The time flies by. They show me pictures of our friends at school that they took during recess. I see the playground and the tetherball and my classmates being silly and smiling and waving to me. Bridget-Ann is riding piggyback on Ms. Benson. We laugh because that is so Bridget-Ann. As they catch me up on all the jokes, projects, and funny moments at school, I play with the squishy cupcake. I feel my fingers sinking into the cupcake and springing back as it returns to its normal shape. My friends tell me how my homeroom is preparing a surprise for me and how the fourth graders are making get-well cards for me and praying for me. It feels good to know they haven't forgotten about me. I'm so sad when Rachel and Amelia leave.

I'm alone again in my silent room, with a "nice" view of the parking lot and the busy road below. The sun is setting. I watch all the cars zipping out of the lot, the drivers rushing to get home to their lives. I wonder what that will feel like—leaving the hospital.

Reflection

I was starting to feel reconnected to my buddies and to my life again. When I felt like I was drowning in my sadness and loneliness in the hospital, I realized my friends buoyed me and kept my head above water. It felt like that time when I was six years old and got knocked over by a huge wave in Pusan Beach, South Korea. My dad had to pull me back onto the beach. Okay, so I wasn't exactly drowning; my dad said I was screaming when I got knocked down, mostly because the salt water burned my mouth and throat. (My dad said I can sometimes be a little dramatic.) The point I'm making is that it was nice to have someone lift me up in my moment of need. When I really needed the help, my friends were there to lift me up.

Week 3, Day 5: **Teaching Love**

> An awesome teacher is hard
> to find, difficult to part with,
> and impossible to forget.
>
> —Unknown

As I lie in bed all day, I think about all the visits I've had. Whenever someone walks through the door, it's almost as if my whole body fills with energy and strength. I grow deeper bonds with all the people who visit, especially my teachers.

I'm more alert now, so I'm more aware of the changes in my life and feel more self-conscious. When Mr. Backer, my school principal, knocks on the door of my room, I remember feeling excitement and nervousness at the same time. What would he think of me, sitting here with all these tubes and lines in me? How would he approach me? Had he seen anyone in the hospital before? Questions piled up into a mountain inside my head.

My worries quickly fade away when Mr. Backer sees past the tubes and machines and treats me like my old self, as if nothing has really changed. I am still the same girl who arrived at the lower school each morning, giving him a high five. He shares hilarious stories from school. He describes how my friends performed a lunchtime jalapeno-eating contest in support of me, which makes me smile because I can definitely see them doing something crazy like that. Mr. Backer also explains that they miss me during the annual lower and middle school spelling bee. Last year, I had gotten second place! That was so much fun. I can still hear my classmates cheering for me. Bummer I'm missing it this year.

My reading teacher, Ms. Parker, also comes to visit. Just like Mr. Backer, she walks into my room with enthusiastic energy that makes me smile. Although I am happy to see her, I long to be back in her classroom, reading and discussing books. She explains what happens next in our class read-aloud, *Tiger Rising* by Kate Dicamillo. Kate Dicamillo is one of my favorite authors, so I am so excited to hear more about her book. I wish I could be at school to hear the rest of the story with my class, discussing the character's decisions and sharing our own personal connections. We use sign language to indicate that we feel the same way when someone shares an idea about the book. We make fists with our thumbs and pinkies pointed up and move them back and forth between ourselves and the other person. I miss doing that.

"Ms. Taylor will be here very soon, Nell," my dad tells me. My mind shifts to the present. I wonder how all my teachers have time to visit me. My mom and my dad alternate staying with me in the hospital; today, it's my dad's turn. Ms. Taylor has been my homeroom teacher since third grade. When she moved up to be a fourth-grade teacher this year, I was lucky enough to have her again! I feel like we have known each other forever. We know how to make each other laugh and smile. I'm excited to see her today because I could really use more laughter.

The knock on my door startles me. "Hi, Nell!" she exclaims. "I'm so happy to see you." My eyes shift upward to look at her face hovering over mine. I smile, and she smiles back, squeezing my hand. "I brought this with me," she says as she holds up a book: *The Wild Robot*.

"That's what we're reading in class!" I exclaim—or at least try to in my groggy voice. Ms. Taylor knows me so well. She knows I hate missing anything in school, let alone a good book. She opens the book and starts to read. "The lonely robot starts to look around …" Her voice becomes a soft and sweet melody that is lulling me to sleep.

"He-llo, Nell," I hear the robotic voice say. Wait a minute. Am I in this story? I suddenly open my eyes. Nobody is in the room. I'm in the same old bed. No robot. No Ms. Taylor. I must have fallen asleep while she was reading. But I know I didn't imagine her visit because I can still feel her warmth in the room.

Reflection

Seeing my teachers in the hospital was really special. They made me laugh and helped me remember how much I love a good story. My connection with them became even stronger than it was before, and I became closer to them. When I eventually returned to school, the transition seemed easier because I didn't need to explain myself. They got it.

Week 3, Day 6: **Cornhole!**

A bad attitude is the only true handicap.

—Scott Hamilton

Over the next few days, I start to perform different kinds of therapy: speech, physical, and occupational therapy. Today I wake up and see that I have "physical therapy" written on my board. Ugh. I kind of hate physical therapy (a.k.a., PT), mainly because I had a bad experience with one therapist. She was grumpy and didn't have any confidence in me. When I was with her, I felt disabled. Mom notices the dread in my eyes. "I just heard that Kat may be coming soon," she announces. This possibility fills me with bubbles of excitement.

"Really?" I want to make sure this is true. Mom nods and I can tell that she's telling the truth. Kat is definitely a way better physical therapist than the ones I've encountered so far, and she's not even trained to be one. I think Mom reads my mind because then she tells me, "Kat isn't going to be your physical therapist today, Nell, but she is going to be there to cheer you on!" *Aw, man!*

"But am I gonna have the same PT person I had last time?" I am really hoping she says no. Last time, when Jake visited me during PT, that therapist held me back from him! I tried to break free from her tight grip on my shoulders and waist so I could give him a hug, but then I felt her fingers clawing me back as if I were a dog on a leash. I got really mad and bonked my head into her shoulder. It was my only way to communicate my anger because I couldn't speak.

"I think you will have a different therapist today," my mom replies. *Yes!* "I heard that she is a really good therapist too." Hmm, I have my doubts, but Kat's presence will definitely make therapy more fun.

"When is it going to be?" I ask. I want to know if I have time to relax.

"In about an hour or so." Okay, that means I will have a little time to myself. I slowly move my arm to grab the remote from my bedside, and I manage to click on the Food Network. Man, I'm addicted to this channel; my favorite show of all time is the Kids Baking Championship, and guess what? That's what's showing! I watch the episode where the kids are baking heavenly eclairs. Yum. I wish I could grab one through the screen, but even then I wouldn't be capable of eating it. Right as the contestants say goodbye to the girl who got eliminated from the competition, I hear a knock at the door.

Mom opens the door, and I immediately hear Kat's bright, loud voice. "Hey, kid, what's up?" I don't even have a chance to answer because Kat immediately introduces Latisha, my physical therapist for the day, whom she has just met outside my room. "Latisha is pretty awesome!" exclaims Kat.

My eyes shift over to look at Latisha. She has a grin on her face, a real grin, and kind, purposeful eyes. Well, if Kat says she's good, then she's probably good.

"All right, Nell, you ready to start?" Latisha asks, not wasting a moment. She already has my walker and wheelchair with her. I nod. What else am I supposed to do? So Latisha takes off my covers, and the nurse detaches me from my IV and a monitor that checks my heart and breathing rate. Eventually, they work together to get me out of bed.

I am now "standing up" with the help of Latisha, Kat, my mom, and my walker (I despise needing so much help). All four of them help me inch out of my room and into the hallway. Latisha helps me walk around the corner with my walker but then allows me to push the walker on my own. "Oh yeah, Nell!" they yell together. Even though I'm so tired, their encouragement pushes me forward. I keep trying to push my body to walk farther and farther. Kat, Latisha, and I have smiles on our faces. This is the first time I have walked without someone holding my body. I feel like I'm flying, even though I've only moved a few feet. I feel a sense of power and hope. Maybe, just maybe, I will be able to return to that lacrosse field one day.

After walking around for what seems like hours, I get to try out one of my favorite games—cornhole! Well, kind of. Latisha has to hold me steady as I stand up from the wheelchair. She hands me the beanbag, and I try to toss it into the hole. It's so much harder than I thought. At first the beanbag slips out of my hand and lands by my feet. "Nell, are you sure you aren't getting too tired?" Latisha questions. I just shake my head. My whole body and mind are determined to get this red beanbag into that hole. I focus hard as I release the beanbag from my hand and watch it go up and then … flop into the hole! Kat, Latisha, and my mom cheer for me. It feels good, but at the same time I feel silly, like a toddler who has just taken her first step. I'm still really proud of myself. I decide to do it again.

"Nell, do you want to go back to your room?" they ask me. I shake my head vigorously and reach my shaky arms out toward Kat, asking for the beanbag. "Okay, Nell! Do you want the beanbag?" Kat looks at me with cautious excitement. I look up at her and nod my head. Kat picks up the red beanbag and slowly hands it to me. I smile. Kat smiles back.

This time I don't let anybody hold me up, but I am partially leaning against my parked wheelchair to steady myself. Then I swing my arm and toss the beanbag up. My eyes track the beanbag's trajectory as it flies through the air in what seems like slow motion. My ears can hear voices, but I can't make out what they're saying because I'm too focused on watching the beanbag. It lands one centimeter just above the hole, then slides in. I hold my breath. When it finally drops into the hole, my right arm flies up like I just won a marathon. My left arm keeps holding onto the wheelchair. "Nell, you scared us there!" they tell me. Exhausted, I collapse into my wheelchair with beads of sweat on my forehead, but I'm happy.

"You're gettin' stronger!" Kat exclaims with her enthusiastic smile. Her whole face lights up. Mine does too.

After finishing PT with some bed exercises like throwing a big pillow (which I like), I am thoroughly exhausted and Latisha leaves. I hug Kat and ask her to say hi to the team for me. As soon as the door closes, my eyelids feel heavy and I fall asleep.

Reflection

Recovering from any hardship takes hard work. Believe in yourself and welcome the support from those who want to help. These tools will help you do more than you think you can.

I had to reach deep down into myself to pull out my true inner determination. It's a strength that I didn't even realize I had until I found it. I guess that's the gift of struggling: discovering the superpowers deep down inside you.

Week 4, Day 1: **Feeling Normal Again**

> When I let go of what I am, I
> become what I might be.
>
> —Lao Tzu

I am worried that I am not the kid I was just a few weeks ago. I've become more aware of everything; I'm aware that I'm different now. I wonder how my friends will react to seeing me this way.

Memories of sprinting down the lacrosse field with the ball in my stick, blowing by defenders, and scoring a powerful goal feel more and more distant. I was strong and confident and happy back then. Now, I am stuck lying in a hospital bed with an inflamed brain and weak body. All these thoughts start to build up like blocks forming a wall inside my head, causing me to forget the capable person I once was. The wall grows so big that I can't see any way around it. My eyes close, and I fall into a deep sleep.

I wake up to knocking on the door and sit up in my bed. My friend Cara from lacrosse and her mom peek their heads into my room. I smile and sit up straighter. They bring a box of cookies that look delicious. I know I can't eat them, so we decide to give them to the nurses. Cara gives me a hug and acts like nothing is different even though I know it's all different. It must be weird for her to see me lying in a hospital bed with an IV in my arm and a heart monitor hovering over my head. The last time we saw each other, we were passing a lacrosse ball and chatting about tryouts and the team. She shares that she wants to make the team again with me next year. I want that too. I remember what it felt like to pass to her and click our sticks together when she scored—pure exhilaration and joy. I want to feel that again.

Her calm smile puts me at ease, and I know I don't have to do or say anything to make her feel comfortable. That's Cara. It's funny how some friends can be themselves with you no matter what.

After I nap, I hear another knock at the door. My friend Eliza is here! She brings me a poster signed by the entire University of Maryland women's lacrosse team! I'm so touched that Eliza and my other lacrosse friend, Zadie, stood in line waiting to get this poster signed for me. It says things like "Get well soon, Nell! Terps are behind you!" I wish I could have stood in line with them and met the team, but having them do this for me is a close second.

After Eliza and I chat about the Maryland lacrosse game and how we both love Caroline Steele, one of the team's best attackers, I learn about Eliza's passion for Michael Jackson. We start joking around about how we love to do funny dances to "Beat It" and "Thriller" and so many more. She even shows me her moonwalk, lifting up her heels one after the other in a fluid motion across the floor—she is so good at it! Then my dad attempts to do it, but he ends up stumbling over his heels, which makes everyone burst into laughter.

After Eliza leaves, I ask my dad to hang the Maryland lacrosse poster in my hospital room. He pins it on the wall opposite my bed. As I go to sleep at night, it's the last thing I see; every morning afterward, it's the first thing I see. It gives me strength. And hope. One day, I'll be sprinting down that lacrosse field with the ball in my stick again.

Reflection

After I saw my friends, I realized they just wanted to see me and didn't have any expectations about who I should be. In fact, they were just relieved to see that I wanted to see them. I'm glad they chose to come visit.

If you ever feel like you want to do something for someone, do it. When it comes from your heart, you will probably make someone feel really good. And that good feeling never goes away.

Week 4, Day 2: **Dogs and Art**

Animals are such agreeable friends. They
ask no questions, they pass no criticisms.

—George Eliot

My eyes open today to see something new planned
on my whiteboard—actually, two new things. I read that
I will have art therapy and a dog visit. Huh, that sounds
cool. Anything with the words *art* or *dog* usually excite
me. Mom notices me eyeing the board. "Exciting day,
huh?" she asks. I nod and smile at her. But then I give her
a questioning look. She assures me that I will enjoy these
activities and explains that art therapy isn't like respiratory
therapy or occupational therapy. In art therapy, she says,
I can squish clay and use art supplies to be creative. I'm
excited. Art is one of my favorite classes at school and now
I finally get a chance to do it here! Geez, why didn't they
tell me about this sooner?

"When can I get started?" I ask.

"In a little over an hour," my mom replies. I lean my bed back by pushing a special button. I relax, and as soon as my head touches the pillow, my eyelids close and I'm fast asleep. Again.

I hear my mom's voice along with another voice I don't recognize as they enter my room. My eyelids open a crack so I can survey my situation before fully waking up. My eyes scan the room and stop suddenly on a cart with colors. I jolt awake to inspect the cart full of fun—a relative term within the white, sterile walls of a hospital.

"Oh, Nell! You're awake!" my mom exclaims. "This is Sean, your art therapist." He wheels the art cart over to my bed and sets up a table over my lap.

"So which supplies do you want to use today?" he asks with a smile. My eyes scan the colorful options. I want to use everything, but I don't think I can. I lift my finger to point to the markers, the pastels, the paint, and the collaging kit. I think this is the hardest decision I've had to make in the hospital so far.

"It seems like you want to use them all!" he exclaims with a laugh. "How about we start with the markers?" I nod. I just want to start. Sean picks a few markers and a piece of paper and places them on the table. My fingers try to grasp the marker, but I can't get a strong enough grip to draw a picture. The next few minutes proceed like this: grasp, fumble, drop, repeat. I want to throw the marker across the room, but I can't. Seeing my frustration, Sean hands me a piece of clay. "You can use the markers to color your clay," he explains. This is much easier. I slowly move the tip of the marker back and forth across the blob of clay in my hands. I get lost in the slowness and quietness of this movement. It's kind of peaceful and relaxing. I forget Sean is still in the room until he asks how I'm doing. Slightly startled, I look up and tell him I'm fine. Then I ask him if we can make slime next time. He can't understand me at first, but I say it louder. "Oh, slime. Sure we can. You aren't the first kid to request that."

Before the hospital, I made slime with my friends, felt that goo between my fingers, and pulled it apart between my hands like taffy. My fingers were strong then. I remember putting food dye and glitter and tiny beads into the slime to change its texture and make it more fun. My friends and I would make a huge mess in the kitchen and would have to clean it all up, but it was always worth it.

Working with my hands again feels good. The art therapy session flies by, and Sean says he has to leave for his next session but leaves the markers and clay.

My mom tells me that I can rest because I'm scheduled to have a dog therapy session in a few hours. The hospital has trained dogs who visit the sick kids and cheer them up. I'm excited but also tired, so I lean back and drift off to sleep as soon as my head hits the pillow.

A woman knocks and sticks her head in to see if it's a good time for a visit. My mom nods and welcomes the woman into my room. I hear little nails clicking on the floor of my room and realize they are on the paws of

35

a medium-sized dog that is approaching my bed. I'm so excited. The woman with the dog first insists that everyone clean their hands with the antibacterial soap before touching the dog so we don't spread germs to other kids. Hearing this, I motion my hand expectantly. My mom laughs and places a little soap into the palm of my right hand. After I carefully rub the soap between my hands, she helps me sit up in my bed so I can get a better look at the dog. He looks like a mini Lassie, with brown and white fur and a long pointy nose. The woman says the dog can jump onto my bed and sit beside me, so I try to scoot my body over, but I need help. The dog jumps onto my bed gingerly. His paws barely graze my left leg. He shifts his weight a little before he settles down, places his face on my thigh, and looks up at me with his cute doggy eyes. Stroking his fur calms me in a way I haven't felt before in my entire hospital stay. I close my eyes, and we both take a nap. Lying next to this dog reminds me of my bunny and the way her soft fur feels against my chest and face as we cuddle on the living room couch at home. I pretend I'm with her.

Reflection

While my physical recovery required hard work, my mind and spirit also needed to heal, and using my hands to create art and feeling the love of an animal helped me heal. I still use art and the love of my pets to boost my spirits.

Week 4, Day 3:
Best Milkshake Ever

Sometimes bad things have to
happen before good things can.

—Becca Fitzpatrick

My health and overall strength start to improve, so I am able to do some more things now, such as talking. Though it's still not exactly clear what I'm saying, people still talk to me, and I'm more attentive to what they're saying. But the thing that I'm really happy about is finally being able to use an actual bathroom!

Before, I would have to use a bedside commode. The nurses had to pick me up and place me on the commode to use it. Not fun at all! But that definitely beat the bedpan. I don't want to go into all of the details of this, but I would basically have to "go" while lying in bed. Now I can, with help, walk to use the bathroom in my room. This is a huge milestone.

Today, I wake up early in the morning with an urge to use the bathroom, so I call for my mom to help me walk. She is pretty much an expert at helping me get up and dragging the IV pole to the bathroom, so I'd rather not have someone else do it.

I am so desperate to just rush out of my bed to relieve myself that, when my mom comes to help me get out, my body jerks upward a bit too fast. The feeding tube that goes through my nose and into my stomach gets caught on the side rail of my bed, and the tube gets pulled out entirely.

"Ouch!" I gag. "Mom!"

"Oh boy," my mom says with a worried look on her face. The sour taste of small amounts of my stomach's contents that get pulled up with the tube from my stomach irritates my throat and mouth. It's gross.

"It's not my fault! It got caught when I tried to get up!" I wail as my eyes focus on the long tube that was just used to feed me.

"It's going to be okay," Mom says reassuringly.

A few minutes later, my nurse walks into the room. "Her feeding tube got caught on the rail," says Mom with a sigh.

"She'll just have to get her appetite back then," the nurse replies in a matter-of-fact tone. "I'll let Dr. Smith know."

"Well, Nell, you can eat whatever you want now," Dr. Smith says a few minutes later with a foreboding look on her face. "As long as you have at least eight hundred calories a day, we don't have to drop another tube down your throat," she tells me. I gulp. That's so many calories! I haven't eaten so much in what seems like months.

"That is a lot of calories, Nell," Mom says. Has she just read my mind?

"I know," I reply with a sigh.

"So that is why I recommend Pediasure," Dr. Smith announces with a smile. "Pediasure is a shake that will give you many nutrients and will help you get lots of calories. I'll go check if we have some. Vanilla, chocolate, or strawberry, Nell?"

"Vanilla," I mumble, concentrating on the stethoscope around her neck and refusing to meet her eye.

"Okay, I'll be right back." She walks out of the room.

About ten minutes later, Dr. Smith comes back into my room with many bottles of Pediasure.

"Here it is," she says as she puts them down on the table. Then she tells me to drink some now. *Seriously? Now?*

"That is a good idea, Nell," my mom agrees. She pops open the bottle for me. I take a whiff of it. Eh, not my number-one choice of smell, but not awful either.

My mom holds the bottle while I take a sip. The taste is like nothing I've tasted before—kind of metallic—and I practically gag on it. Mom just sighs when she glances at me. "Nell, you really are going to need to drink this if you don't want another tube down your throat," she tells me. My eyes shift down to look at the nasty drink. *Gosh, why are things so unfair? When will all of this end?* My negative thoughts are suddenly interrupted by a knock at the door.

"Hello! It's so great to see you!" A kind voice fills the room. Immediately, the sound of my amazing writing teacher, Ms. Benson, sweeps away any negative thoughts lingering in my head. Her smiling face emerges from behind the curtain surrounding my bed. Even better, she's holding something: a *huge* milkshake! It is the size of a Big Gulp from 7-Eleven with a huge straw and whipped cream dripping down the side. I can't even speak. I'm so amazed, confused, excited, and grateful all at once. "That's right, Nell. I brought you this since I knew that you would be able to swallow it easily." Ms. Benson didn't know that I had accidentally pulled out my feeding tube, but the amazing timing of her arrival with that milkshake felt like a small miracle.

"You know, Nell, we could put the Pediasure in the milkshake!" my mom tells me. I eagerly nod my head in agreement.

Once my mom dumps the disgusting shake into the delicious milkshake, I start to drink with delight. Thick, fluffy clouds of sweet vanilla goodness fill my mouth and coat my throat. I don't even taste the Pediasure. I suddenly remember how good a milkshake tastes and how good it feels to eat or drink something for real, not through a tube.

Reflection

Ms. Benson brought me more than just the delicious, high-calorie milkshake. Being able to drink it on my own saved me from the torture of getting another feeding tube placed. Ms. Benson came to visit just when I needed her the most. She was definitely one of my angels.

Look for the angels in your life. They could come at unexpected times, and you might be surprised by who they are. Open yourself to the light that they bring.

Week 4, Day 5: **Mighty Mom Saves the Day!**

> I may not have gone where I
> intended to go, but I think I ended
> up where I intended to be.
>
> —Douglas Adams

I am going to ride in an ambulance today, and I'm honestly really excited about it! I've never been in an ambulance before; I've only heard their loud sirens and played with miniature toy versions. I'm also excited for a change of scenery. According to my mom, I will be leaving this medical hospital to go to a rehabilitation hospital, where they will put me through exercises meant to make me stronger. I wonder if there will be other kids like me at this new hospital.

As thoughts of this new change drift in and out of my mind, I suddenly hear my mom's voice harshly speaking to a doctor.

"If Nell can't go today, then why—"

"I'm sorry, but this is a holiday weekend and we ..." The doctor's voice trails off.

What is happening? Why am I unable to leave today? Will I just have to wait helplessly in this bed until I am allowed to leave? The last of my excitement drains rapidly as I strain my ears to hear more. All I can hear are faint whispers.

After they talk for what feels like an eternity, I learn from my mom that today is a holiday weekend, President's Day to be exact, and there isn't a way for me to be admitted to the rehab hospital, let alone get there. No ambulance ride either.

"So I guess I *do* have to stay here longer," I mumble with my head down, biting my lip.

"Actually, I am trying to convince them to let you leave today." Even though my mom's words are faint, there is a strong determination in her voice.

"Leave? Leave where?" I pause, holding my breath. "Home?" And right as I whisper that warm, comforting word that I haven't let myself say in ages, I realize that my mom is saying that same word. For a moment, we are both thinking deeply, remembering something; we are remembering home. My mom and I suddenly are connecting in a deeper way, where we both understand the pain, emotion, thoughts, and memories of this very moment.

Suddenly, there is a knock at the door. I hear a faint creak as a man with a clipboard steps into my room. He begins to speak to my mom, and they keep talking for what seems like hours about boring medical stuff. Finally, when they're finished, the man hands my mom his clipboard.

"I will need you to sign these papers, and then you'll be able to take her home," he tells my mom.

I have never felt so excited. *I am going home. Home. Home!* The word has never meant so much in my whole life.

My mom eagerly signs off on the gazillion papers attached to the clipboard. I hear the pen scribble vigorously against the pages until Mom puts the pen down and hands the guy his clipboard. He flips through the forms to make sure she completed them all and announces, "You're practically all set, so—"

"Thank you so much," Mom interrupts loudly and begins to shoo him politely out the door. As soon as he leaves, she starts to pack up all our belongings. Every colorful card, gift, and treat is placed in a large bag. Any extra clothes, food, and supplies are also packed up.

The nurses and my mom start disconnecting me from all the tubes and wires. My IV, my heart rate monitor, my blood pressure cuff—all the things that kept me bound to this bed for so long are taken off. My hospital wristband came off too, one of the things defining my identity until now. Without depending on these machines, I'm finally free to return to my true self. To return home.

My mom helps me change out of the scratchy hospital scrubs and into some soft, clean clothes and warm, fuzzy boots. Soon enough, we're all ready to go, but there's just one issue: even though I've gotten much stronger, I am still not coordinated enough to walk all the way to the car. Many of the nurses as well as my mom notice my weakness, and they provide me with a wheelchair.

As I am wheeled down these hospital halls for the last time, many of my nurses say goodbye. I glimpse at the faces of some of the other kids who are staying in the same area of the hospital as me.

Why can't all of the other kids experience this freedom too? I think as we exit the hall. It feels wrong to be leaving when all the other kids have to stay.

When we finally reach the car and begin to drive away, I start to feel like I am leaving a part of myself behind and becoming someone new. I also find myself thinking about how good it will feel to see my brother and eat dinner with my family again, and I just can't wait to sleep in my own bed.

Soon enough, we pull into our driveway and my mom pushes a button clipped to the sun visor above her head to open the garage. Slowly and steadily, she helps me out of my seat, and together we inch into the house.

When we finally reach the top of the basement stairs and enter the main floor, I am immediately greeted by the aroma of homemade tomato sauce, the smell of coffee brewing in our kitchen, and so many other wonderful, indescribable things I longed to have for so long. With beads of sweat on my forehead, I collapse onto my favorite armchair in the family room. Mom brings Bunnis over and puts her next to me on the armchair.

"Bunnis!" I stroke her soft, gray fur as she settles into her comfy spot on my side. "Mom, are Jake and Dad coming home soon?" I ask. I just can't wait to see them.

"Yes, they should be home any moment now," Mom replies. That's just when I hear the garage open and a car door slam shut.

"They're home!" I cry. I hear my brother running up the stairs. Bursting through the door, he smiles and drops his book bag to come give me a hug. My dad walks in next. His face has the biggest smile I've ever seen, and his eyes look glossy in the light. Immediately, he comes over and scoops me up into a big bear hug. I squeeze him as hard as I can, and he laughs heartily, the one I haven't heard in so long.

We share a nice, warm meal of homemade meatballs and spaghetti with freshly grated parmesan cheese and freshly chopped parsley. As we talk at the dinner table, I realize that even though this isn't the first time since entering the hospital that I am together with my family, it feels like the first time. My parents don't turn away to whisper about me or glance at me worriedly; they speak directly to me, including me in the conversation. My brother shares a funny story from school about a boy who made farty noises in class and was asked to go to the dean. We burst into laughter. We are authentically ourselves.

I finally crawl into my warm, cozy bed. My head sinks into my favorite plush pillow, and I smell a familiar clean, soapy smell as I bury my face into the fluff. I think about all the happiness that I felt today, but I also begin to worry about what I've missed at school and in my life. Now that I'm not in the hospital, I feel like I need to return to my old life again: playing lacrosse, learning cool things at school, and talking and laughing with my friends. Being home makes those things feel within my reach, but I know I still have a long way to go before I get there.

Reflection

Sometimes what we perceive as negative can turn into the most amazing thing. When I wasn't able to go to the rehab hospital that day, I ended up going home! Sometimes we can help to create that positivity, like how my mom convinced the doctor to let me come home.

Look for those flashes of light in the darkness—the people who lift you up. Let them guide you through until, one day, you outshine the dark. You are the light. The darkness never really goes away, but it can't defeat you. Use your brightness to be a light for others.

Epilogue

After I left the hospital, I thought I had endured the worst of my journey and my life would go back to normal, but that was far from the truth. When I got home, I was ecstatic and loved the amazing welcome I got from my family and friends. I was on a high, like having my birthday and Christmas rolled into one. But after about a week of this, the high started to wane. Jake returned to his life at school, and my dad returned to work. My mom, who usually worked at home, was busy taking me to my many occupational and physical therapy appointments and preparing meals so I could get stronger. It was exhausting going back and forth to my appointments and even more exhausting doing the therapies. I struggled to walk, so my mom had to put me in a wheelchair to transport me from the car to the rehab sessions. Someone had to help me get up and down the stairs in my home.

I was both anxious and excited to return to school in mid March. On my first day back, my school principal arranged a big surprise at our morning assembly—me! The kids at my school didn't know that I was returning to school that day. My principal had me wait in the tech room behind the assembly area until he was ready to announce me. When I stepped out of the room, I was greeted by loud cheers and applause from my school friends and teachers. That was awesome.

Receiving many hugs and high fives, I had a great first day back, but I quickly found that I wasn't myself at all. While my friends could run around with endless energy during recess, I felt so tired after my morning classes and needed to nap during the day, so I couldn't even make it to recess. I couldn't interact with my friends the way I had before all this happened—I had changed, and they hadn't. Despite their best efforts, they just hadn't experienced what I had. I felt more alone than ever. I did half days for many weeks and then increased my hours slowly as the year progressed. My school year eventually ended in the beginning of June. I was still tired.

My emotions, energy levels, and overall health in the months after the hospital were inconsistent and unpredictable; it was like being on a crazy roller coaster with steep climbs and sudden drops and unexpected upside-down twists that make your stomach flip—but without the fun. I wish that someone could have warned me about that before I left the hospital.

I also wish I had understood what my brother was going through while I was sick. Looking back on this, I feel so bad. I forgot that he had started a new school in sixth grade and was nervous about taking midterm exams for the first time that winter when I was in the hospital. After school, he came home on the bus to an empty house and had to eat and study alone and maybe wonder how I was doing. How depressing that must have been! He didn't have anyone to relax or laugh with at the end of his day. Thank God Bunnis was with him then!

Oh, that's another thing that happened a month after I got home—Bunnis died. It was kind of sudden. The veterinarian said she had a heart valve problem or something. When I found out my mom had to put her to sleep to end her suffering, I cried and cried at school. Maybe I needed to cry, not just about Bunnis but about everything—the illness that put me in the hospital, the stress that it caused my family, the unexpected changes in my life, the nagging fact that I wasn't the same person I was before and that life would never be the same, either. I finally started to accept that my life was changed for good.

•••

Fast forward two years. I still struggle with fatigue and have an ongoing cough and now an ear infection. This might be because I'm on a medicine that makes my immune system weaker, or at least that's what everyone says. I still don't remember a lot of what happened. Every now and then, I have little flashbacks to my time in the hospital, and I work on processing those memories all over again. I'm learning to accept my story as a part of who I am.

My sickness doesn't define my identity, but it has become a part of it. It has made me the person I am today. And I am proud of who I've become.

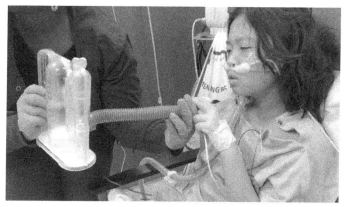

One of the "torture devices"
to help me breathe

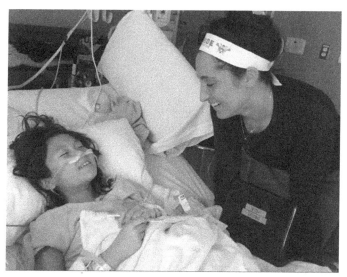

Coach Katie (Kat) teaching me
how to brush my teeth again

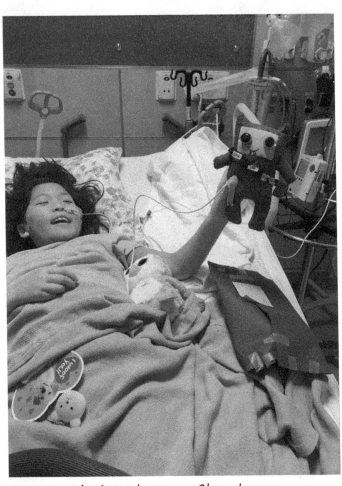

My hand-sewn Chewbacca
gift from a dear friend

One of my favorite furry
hospital companions :)

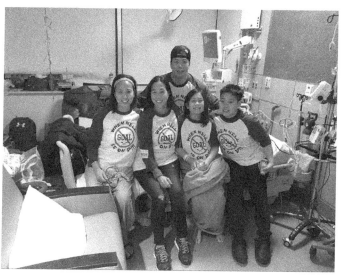

My family and I together on
the eve of discharge

Why I Wrote This Book

When I was sick in the hospital, there were lots of other kids there too. As I walked the halls with my physical therapist or was pushed in my wheelchair, I saw the other kids in their beds with IVs like mine hanging from their arms, watching TV or just lying there. I wanted to talk to them and find out how they felt and what they were thinking. I wanted to hear their stories as much as I wanted to share mine, but I never got a chance.

One of my teachers, Mrs. Claire Norris, gave me a journal to write about my feelings as I transitioned back to school. Writing about my traumatic experience helped me heal and brought me strength when I felt discouraged about not having enough energy to fully participate in the activities I loved before my illness. I wrote to work through my frustration with myself.

That's when I started to write this book.

I hope my story will help the broader community understand what it was like for me to suddenly become really sick, feel alone in a hospital room, not know what would happen to me, and worse, feel like the rest of the world was going on without me. And for those of you who already understand and are going through a similar experience, I want to show you that you aren't alone and that you have a story worth sharing.

I was nine then, and I'm twelve now as I finally complete this book. I'm a little older and stronger, but I'm still a kid. My time in the hospital and living with this disease has changed me—for worse and for better too. Though I expect to live with this disease for the rest of my life (until a cure is discovered, fingers crossed), I've grown a lot from this experience so far. Although I have to miss out on late-night events and have trouble doing physical activities without getting dizzy or feeling sick, I am more grateful for the small things: waking up in my own bed, running outside, roasting marshmallows in the firepit with my family, having snowball fights with Jake, cuddling with my cats, and baking my favorite red velvet cupcakes with cream cheese frosting. Most of all, I continue to be grateful for the people who reached out to me during my time of struggle.

When my mom asked if I could erase all of what happened to me, to my surprise and hers, I said no. The experience has become part of me, my story.

Your life, your story. I have written mine. Now it's time to share yours.

Acknowledgments

To my amazing family, especially my parents, for staying late nights at the hospital and taking days off of work to be by my side and for knowing exactly how to cheer me up. To my brother Jake, for staying strong at home on his own and for making me laugh no matter how down I was.

To all of my grandparents, for checking in on me and including me in their thoughts and prayers. Specifically, to my late grandmother, Soung Youn Lee, for giving me an outlet to share my pain and feelings through journaling. Even though she wasn't physically with me, her spirit helped guide me through some of my toughest days.

To Aunt Mel, for not only visiting and supporting me in the hospital but also for staying with my brother and bringing him food and his favorite mint chocolate chip ice cream while he studied for his 6th grade midterms alone at home.

To all of my doctors, nurses, therapists, and techs (too numerous to name individually) at Children's National Hospital and Inova Children's Hospital, for supporting me throughout and beyond my hospitalization. They are the ones who made the little miracles possible, helping me to become the healthy girl I am.

To my teachers and the broader Holton-Arms community, for sending their unwavering positivity throughout my illness and for giving me the warmest welcome when I was able to join the community again.

To all of the families in the Holton-Arms School community and St. Albans School community who brought delicious meals and love to us during difficult times.

To Younghee Bae, for always knowing what I needed and for showing me pictures of the crazy and strong toddler I was when she was my nanny.

To all of my friends and extended family, for sending me funny videos, creative cards, and tasty baked goods, but mostly for just thinking of me and making me laugh.

To Coach Katie McMahon and my Pride Lacrosse Team and McLean Youth Lacrosse Team, for being the bright energy that lifted me up—including me in their team cheers when I couldn't play with them and sending colorful cards with words of support.

To Lillian Broeksmit, for helping me on my journey

of writing my book by making my ideas come to life and teaching me all about grammar rules, *especially* semicolons.

To Catherine Andrews, for listening and understanding, especially when my frustration and emotional struggles persisted beyond my hospitalization.

To Kathryn Palmer and Don Wright, for supporting me all the way from Santa Fe and for providing the steady voice of reason amid the uncertainty.

To Neha Patel, for making me laugh on Facetime while I was in the hospital and for all the free acupuncture.

To the Children's National Hospital Foundation for supporting me during my hospitalization and for connecting me to the vast network of wonderful people when I wanted to give back. Special thanks to Jean-Marie Fernandez for connecting me to the foundation.

To ShellyAnn Hope, Program Manager for the Nurse Navigation Program at Children's National Hospital, for helping our family communicate with the many doctors taking care of me and for giving me a special blanket to use as background when I was doing virtual school from my hospital room.

To Shannon Powell and Angelica Bowman, Child Life Specialists at Children's National Hospital, for making my time in the hospital magical in the healing garden and for coming to my room dressed up as a giant space alien and making me laugh.

To the Holton-Arms Alumnae Office, for connecting me with alumnae in the publishing world, and to those alums, who provided me with the resources I needed to publish my book.

You are all my angels, those flashes of light in the darkness. From the bottom of my heart, thank you.

CPSIA information can be obtained
at www.ICGtesting.com
Printed in the USA
BVHW030039080321
601957BV00026B/210